LEARNING FROM NATURE

DR. JOHN A. WOOD
3300 NORTH RIDGE DRIVE
WACO, TEXAS, 76710
JohnWoodMinistry@aol.com

SPECIAL THANKS TO:
JOHN WOOD MINISTRIES, INC.
INTERNATIONAL MEDICAL EDUCATON FOUNDATION, INC.

EDITORS: DANA STAIRS & SUSIE JAYNES

AVAILABLE AT AMAZON.COM, CREATESPACE.COM, AND OTHER RETAILERS

CREATESPACE INDEPENDENT PUBLISHING PLATFORM
NORTH CHARLESTON, SOUTH CAROLINA

ISBN 10: 1479168750
ISBN 13: 9781479168750

Other publications by Dr. John A. Wood:
MASTERS OF FEDOSKINO
IVORY CARVING IN NORTHERN RUSSIA
NEW VISIONS OF RUSSIAN LACQUER ART
GOD'S ERRAND BOY *FISHING ON THE OTHER SIDE*

LEARNING FROM NATURE

DR. JOHN ALVIN WOOD

Walking through the woods with my dad, noticing fascinating elements of God's creation, has built treasured memories that remain to this day. I remember the awe I felt standing under a giant oak tree – realizing this magnificent tree started as a tiny acorn. I was fascinated to discover that each tree produces a distinctive bark and leaves.

On one occasion, as I stood close to a large tree, I thought I saw the bark move. I was puzzled how this could be and thought perhaps my eyes were playing tricks on me. Then, I noticed two little yellow eyes. I breathed a sigh of relief to see that the "moving bark" was actually the camouflaged skin of a tree lizard. Daddy told me that God gave him that skin to blend with the bark so he could hide from anything that would harm him. He could also sneak up on an ant, a spider or a caterpillar he might want to eat. His long sticky tongue would shoot out of his mouth and bring back his food.

Later, we saw a green caterpillar eating away at a leaf. Daddy said that the caterpillar better stay away from that lizard who might eat him for dinner. Daddy says that some caterpillars spin a cocoon of silk around themselves. Later, they break out of their cocoon and become beautiful butterflies. We often see gorgeous butterflies in the forest and around the flowers in our garden at home.

Most trees change with the different seasons, losing their leaves in the winter. Before they fall to cover the forest floor, these leaves change color-from green to red or yellow or orange or gold. To capture the memory of their beauty, I collected several, took them home, and placed them between the pages of one of my books. Every time I look at these gorgeous shades I think of our walks in the forest.

These walks also revealed many different species of birds. I discovered that each kind of bird had a distinctive shape, beak, colored feathers, and even different songs. I asked my dad, "Why are the colors on the male birds so much brighter and more vivid than on the female birds? He answered, "That is God's provision – to protect and disguise the female when she is sitting on eggs in her nest."

Daddy and I had an interesting experience last spring. We watched a pair of cardinals build their nest on the patio of our home. Mother has a pair of beautiful bushes planted in concrete pots on our patio. We watched the red birds build their nest in one of those bushes just outside our kitchen window.

Both the momma bird and the daddy bird worked tirelessly, bringing long strands of grass and small twigs to the bush they had chosen. They intricately wove each piece into a nest. Their task required many trips, back and forth, before it was a safe place for the mother bird to lay her eggs.

We checked on the little family almost every day. The mother bird would sit very low in the nest to keep her eggs warm. In a few weeks the little chicks broke out of their eggs and began to beg for food. Both the momma bird and the daddy bird would fly away in search of worms and bugs to feed their hungry little chicks. We continued watching them as the little birds grew and grew. One day a little bird fell out of the nest. Daddy picked up the little bird and put him back into the nest. When they could fly, they left the nest and started life on their own.

We did not disturb the nest in hopes that they might use the same nest again next spring. I will watch to see if they return.

One time we saw a bird's nest in the forest. The momma bird was sitting very low in the nest keeping her eggs warm. As we walked nearer the nest, the momma bird flew away. The nest was low enough in the small tree that we could actually see into it. We could see four little white eggs in the center of the nest.

When the little baby birds are hatched, both the momma bird and the daddy bird search for food to bring to the little ones. When the little birds get older they test their wings. I am sure they have fun when they learn to fly on their own and to search for their own food.

We heard someone hammering in the forest. We wondered who would be building something out in the middle of the forest. We walked toward the hammering sound and it became louder and louder. Our eyes searched a large dead tree, seemingly the source of the noise. We spotted our energetic "carpenter" – a woodpecker, vigorously pounding on the tree bark with his built-in hammer – a strong pointed beak. His long sharp toenails dug into the tree bark, letting him perch on the side of the trunk even though there was no limb to sit on. We could not decide if he were trying to hollow out a hole to serve as his nest site (which is sometimes the case) or if he were digging out an insect within the wood for food.

I asked daddy if the woodpecker got a headache from pecking at the tree so often and so hard. Daddy told me that God made him to be able to peck at the tree like he was doing. We watched him peck away for a long time and then we continued exploring the forest.

Knowing my fascination with birds, daddy helped me build a bird feeder. We hung it on the porch just outside our kitchen window. This allowed me close observations as the different birds came to feed. (Watching birds just beyond the window pane, contrasted to their harried flight whenever I approached them in the forest.) Amazingly, some birds loved to sit on the feeder, while other species always chose to feed on the seed the others had knocked to the ground. I loved seeing blue jays, doves, sparrows, wrens, cardinals, finch, cedar wax wings and black capped chickadees as they enjoyed the food we put out for them.

My daddy is a skilled craftsman and has a small shop in back of our home. He let me help him build a hummingbird feeder and we put some special food in it. Hummingbirds need a special liquid food. That is because their beak is a thin, narrow, curved arc which works almost like a soda straw, and they sip their food. Even though hummingbirds are tiny in size, they act aggressively toward other hummers as they feed, as if they are saying, "This is MY feeder. Go find your own!" Their wings move so fast as to seem invisible, allowing them to hover as they eat. Their feathers seem to glow with a beautiful sheen in the light. Daddy has a book on birds and showed me that each type of hummingbird has different colored feathers.

The hummingbirds and I have become very close friends. I can hold a cup of their special liquid food in my hand and sit very still. The birds will actually sit on my fingers while they drink. I try to feed the hummingbirds like this every day.

Sometimes we walk along the stream and throw bread to feed the fish. It is fun to watch them come to the surface for their food. I would like to touch them and play with them, but they cannot live out of the water for very long. I imagine it would be fun to observe them up close if I could go in the water and watch them swim, but I cannot hold my breath long enough to follow them very far.

We have an aquarium at home. I love to watch the fish swim in and out of the little porcelain castle and among the seaweed as it dances back and forth with the flow of the water. The aerator pump forces air into the water to help the fish breathe and also makes the seaweed move.

We are sometimes lucky to actually see animals that live in the forest. They seem afraid of us and run away when we try to get close to them. I wish I could pet them and even take them home to live at our house. I could feed them and we could become friends if they were not afraid of people. They should not fear me, because I am their friend and I would not hurt them. I would only love them and they would be my very special pets. However, God intended them to live wild and free.

One day we saw a rabbit feeding in the grass. He was so cute, but he ran away as we approached. I would like to have a bunny rabbit for a pet that I could love and hold.

We heard something chattering in the trees. We stood quietly and saw a squirrel out on a limb swishing his bushy tail back and forth. I am sure he was wondering what we were doing entering his world. We saw him take an acorn in his mouth. He used his strong teeth to remove the hard shell of the acorn and then held the inner part in his front feet while he ate it. He was so cute and we watched him for quite awhile. Then, he jumped from an outer limb onto another tree and disappeared from our sight.

On another trip to the forest we saw a baby deer. His hair was light brown with tiny white spots on it. We wondered where his mother was, but surely she was nearby. Then, the young fawn ran into the forest and back to his mother. Young deer stay with their mother until they are older and can live by themselves. Sometimes, they live in groups and play with each other like I do with my friends.

I have learned a lot about the birds and animals that live in the forest and about the fish that live in the lakes and streams. God created marvelous and varied creatures to inhabit His world. He created every living creature to live in a certain way. Birds and animals live in the forest and fish live in the water.

I wonder what would happen if animals tried to live under the water and fish tried to live on land in the forest. Tragic results would follow if they tried to live in ways God never intended for them to live. Animals would drown under the water and fish would die if they tried to live in the forest.

Now, I think about my own life and my friends. God also created us to live in certain ways. He gave us our own power to decide how we are going to live. We are free to make our own decisions. We can live anyway we want, because we are free to choose. However, God made me and my friends to live in certain ways, just as he did the animals in the forest and the fish in the streams and lakes.

Nature taught me that animals cannot live under the water and fish cannot live out of the water. God did not make my lungs to have smoke inside them. I can choose to smoke like some people do, but that is not the way God intended. If they do smoke their lungs will have a hard time staying healthy. In fact, their lungs can quit helping them breathe and they might become very sick or even die.

Daddy told me about some young people taking drugs, but that is not the way God intended for them to live. They are free to try drugs, but something bad will happen if they do. Some people drink alcohol. That is their choice, but it will hurt their bodies in many ways. God did not intend for our bodies to have alcohol in them.

I learned in church that the Bible tells me that I am the most important part of God's creation. The same laws that exist in nature also apply to my life and to the lives of my friends. I am free to live in ways God never intended, but I am not free to avoid the bad things that will happen to me if I do.

Nature has taught me a lot about how I must live every day if I am to be healthy and strong. I am choosing to live like God intended me to live so I will be healthy and strong. God loves me and I want to love Him and to obey Him. So, I am only going to do the things that are pleasing to God and also make my body healthy and strong. I plan to encourage my friends to live like God intended them to live so they will be happy and healthy and have lots of fun when we play together.

www.ingramcontent.com/pod-product-compliance
Lightning Source LLC
Chambersburg PA
CBHW041523280526
45792CB00004B/1355